GLACIERS

Christine Webster

www.av2books.com

MEDIA ENHANCED BOOKS
AV² BY WEIGL
ADDED VALUE • AUDIO VISUAL

BOOK CODE

Y364823

AV² by Weigl brings you media enhanced books that support active learning.

AV² provides enriched content that supplements and complements this book. Weigl's AV² books strive to create inspired learning and engage young minds for a total learning experience.

Go to **www.av2books.com**, and enter this book's unique code. You will have access to video, audio, web links, quizzes, a slide show, and activities.

Audio
Listen to sections of the book read aloud.

Video
Watch informative video clips.

Web Link
Find research sites and play interactive games.

Try This!
Complete activities and hands-on experiments.

Due to the dynamic nature of the Internet, some of the URLs and activities provided as part of AV² by Weigl may have changed or ceased to exist. AV² by Weigl accepts no responsibility for any such changes. All media enhanced books are regularly monitored to update addresses and sites in a timely manner. Contact AV² by Weigl at 1-866-649-3445 or av2books@weigl.com with any questions, comments, or feedback.

Published by AV² By Weigl
350 5th Avenue, 59th Floor
New York, NY 10118
Website: www.av2books.com   www.weigl.com

Library of Congress Cataloging-in-Publication Data

Webster, Christine.
 Glaciers : water science / Christine Webster.
    p. cm.
 Includes bibliographical references and index.
 ISBN 978-1-61690-000-7 (hardcover : alk. paper) -- ISBN 978-1-61690-006-9 (softcover : alk. paper) -- ISBN 978-1-61690-012-0 (e-book : alk. paper)
 1. Glaciers--Juvenile literature. 2. Water--Juvenile literature. I. Title.
 GB2403.8.W453 2011
 551.31'2--dc22

                        2009052078

Printed in the United States of America in North Mankato, Minnesota
1 2 3 4 5 6 7 8 9 0 14 13 12 11 10

052010
WEP264000

Project Coordinator Heather C. Hudak
Design Terry Paulhus

Photo Credits
Every reasonable effort has been made to trace ownership and to obtain permission to reprint copyright material. The publishers would be pleased to have any errors or omissions brought to their attention so that they may be corrected in subsequent printings.

Weigl acknowledges Getty Images as its primary image supplier for this title.
National Snow and Ice Data Center: Pages 12–13 map source.

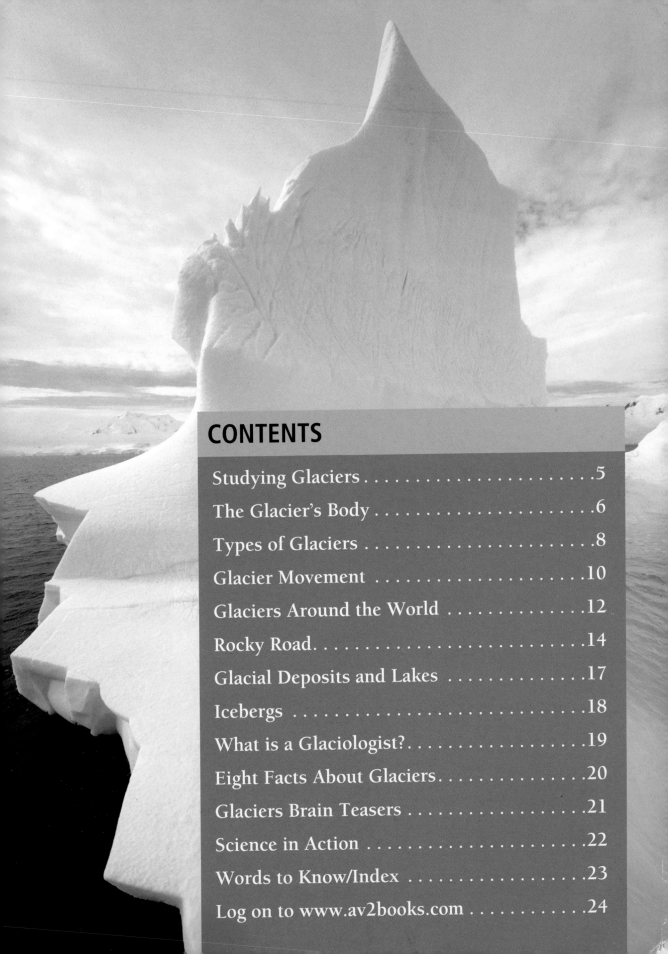

CONTENTS

Global warming is the increase in Earth's temperature due to **greenhouse gases**. It is one of the main reasons glaciers are retreating. Using less energy helps stop global warming. Turning off lights, televisions, or computers when they are not in use, using a fan instead of air conditioning, taking shorter showers, walking or biking short distances instead of driving, and planting trees are just a few of the ways people can help stop global warming.

Studying Glaciers

A large mass of ice in a very cold region is called a glacier. Glaciers form in areas where it is so cold that snow does not melt. Layers of snow build up over many years and become ice. Glaciers can be as large as an entire **continent**. They can also fill a small valley between mountains. Over time, the glacier's weight and **gravity** cause it to move. Most glaciers move very slowly.

Glaciers only form in certain conditions. Snow falls in very cold, moist air. Snow is light and fluffy when it first falls. As more snow falls, the air in the bottom layer of snow disappears. The snow becomes ice. In very cold **climates**, thick layers of ice build up. The ice's weight and gravity cause it to move, or flow. The ice becomes a glacier.

Glacial ice covers about 10 percent of Earth's land area. Most of this glacial ice formed about 5,000 years ago. Glaciers currently cover 5.8 million square miles (15 million square kilometers) of Earth.

In Iceland, glaciers cover about 11.5 percent of the country's landscape. That is an area of 4,536 square miles (11,750 sq. km). Iceland's largest glacier is bigger than the state of Rhode Island.

The Glacier's Body

Most glaciers have three areas. The first area is where a glacier grows larger by collecting snowfall. This area is called the accumulation zone. Here, snow piles up on the upper part of the glacier.

The second area is called the ablation zone. Ablation is the loss of snow, ice, and water from a glacier. In this area, glaciers become smaller as snow melts and **evaporates**. More material is lost than added in the lower part of a glacier.

The area between the accumulation zone and the ablation zone is called the equilibrium zone. Very little snow, ice, or water is added or lost in this area.

GLACIER ZONES

❶ The accumulation zone is found here.

❷ This is the ablation zone.

❸ The equilibrium zone is located here.

❹ As the ice moves, it scrapes the ground below. The scrapings form a ridge at the front of the glacier.

❺ Sometimes, a second glacier becomes part of the main flow.

❻ When the two flows meet, they form a single flow along the center of the glacier. This may give the glacier a striped look.

❼ Chunks of ice break off as the main glacier melts.

❽ Near the endpoint of the glacier, the ice thins. Cracks form.

❾ Melted ice, or meltwater, flows through channels and tunnels.

❿ Water blends with snow to create a thick ice bed.

⓫ The glacier bed is made up of rock and gravel.

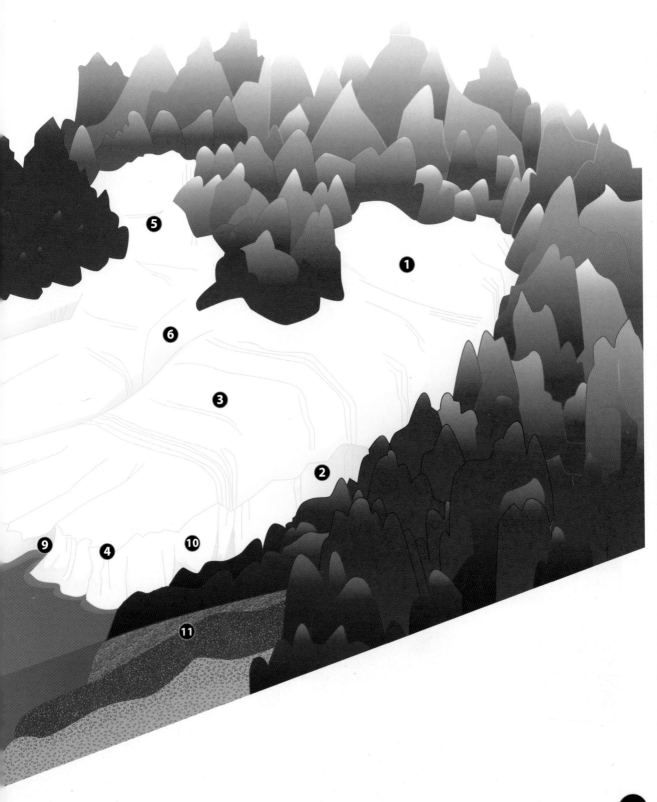

Types of Glaciers

Glaciers can be grouped and sorted in different ways. One way to group them is based on their size. There are three sizes.

ICE SHEETS

- The largest ice masses on Earth
- Usually cover vast land areas
- The Antarctic Ice Sheet spreads across 5 million square miles (13 million sq. km) and is more than 14,000 feet (4 km) thick.

ICECAPS

- Smaller than ice sheets
- Found in Alaska, the Canadian Arctic, Greenland, Iceland, and Norway
- When icecaps grow thick, ice overflows and travels down through glaciers in valleys.

ICE FIELDS

- Form where mountain peaks and ridges push through glaciers in valleys
- Are common in Alaska
- One ice field can cover 1,500 square miles (4,000 sq. km).

Glaciers can also be grouped by their location. The chart below shows three places where glaciers are found.

VALLEY GLACIERS

- Form from icecaps high in mountains
- Easily **erode** the landscape
- Create U-shaped valleys
- Can be up to 3,000 feet (914 m) thick and 100 miles (161 km) long

ALPINE GLACIERS

- Sometimes called mountain or cirque glaciers
- A cirque is a rounded, bowl-shaped area where snow collects.
- Located high in the mountains
- Are smaller than valley glaciers
- Ice easily flows over the cirque and travels down mountains into valleys.
- Can cause **avalanches**

PIEDMONT GLACIERS

- Located at the bottom of mountain ranges
- Are wide and round
- Form when valley glaciers flow over lower mountain slopes and spread out

Glacier Movement

Glaciers move in two different ways. One way is to slide. The other way is to creep. Sometimes, ice layers slide past each other. For instance, if a bottom layer melts, a thin layer of water forms where the ice was. This allows the glacier to slide more easily. This is called sliding.

The other form of movement is called creep. The glacier is so heavy that ice layers form on top of other ice layers. The weight of the top layers changes the glacier's shape inside. The weight also causes the glacier to move.

Glaciers move faster or slower depending on the season, how much snow falls, and the glacier's mass. If a glacier moves too quickly, the ice can crack. Some glaciers move more than 100 feet (30 meters) per day. Other glaciers only move about 6 inches (15 centimeters) per day. In 1827, a Swiss scientist placed a hut on a glacier. When he returned three years later, the hut had moved 100 yards (91 m) downhill.

■ A rise in temperature over the past 50 years has caused about 84 percent of Antarctica's glaciers to decrease in size. The glaciers have decrease an average of 1,970 feet (600 m).

Glacier Movement Over Time

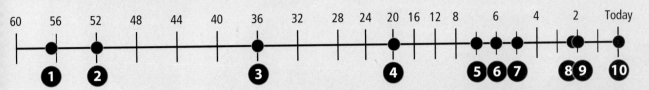

60   56   52   48   44   40   36   32   28   24   20   16   12   8   6   4   2   Today

① 57 to 52 million years ago
Earth's climate is fairly warm.

② 52 to 36 million years ago
Icecaps form in East Antarctica. Near Antarctica, the surface water temperature is only 41 to 46 degrees Fahrenheit (5 to 8 degrees Celsius).

③ 36 to 20 million years ago
Earth begins cooling. A large ice sheet forms on east Antarctica. Average temperatures drop by about 54°F (12°C) in North America, while glaciers appear in Antarctica.

④ 20 to 16 million years ago
Earth's climate cools even more.

⑤ 7 million years ago
All of Greenland is covered by glaciers.

⑥ 6 to 5 million years ago
Glaciers extend to Scandinavia and parts of the north Pacific region.

⑦ 5 to 3 million years ago
Sea temperatures around North America and Antarctica are warmer than present-day temperatures.

⑧ 2.5 million years ago
Tundra takes over north-central Europe, while grasslands replace lush landscapes in central China and parts of Africa.

⑨ 2 million to 14,000 years ago
Large glacial ice sheets cover most of North America, Europe, and Asia for long periods of time. These glaciers retreat as the climate warms.

⑩ 14,000 years ago to today
Glaciers continue to retreat.

Glaciers Around the World

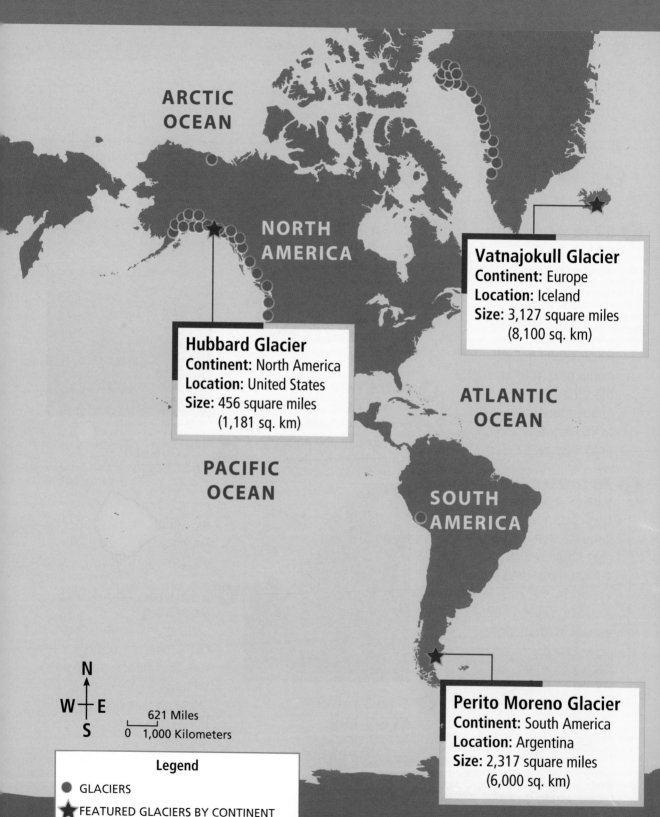

ARCTIC OCEAN

NORTH AMERICA

Vatnajokull Glacier
Continent: Europe
Location: Iceland
Size: 3,127 square miles
(8,100 sq. km)

Hubbard Glacier
Continent: North America
Location: United States
Size: 456 square miles
(1,181 sq. km)

ATLANTIC OCEAN

PACIFIC OCEAN

SOUTH AMERICA

N
W E
S

621 Miles
0   1,000 Kilometers

Perito Moreno Glacier
Continent: South America
Location: Argentina
Size: 2,317 square miles
(6,000 sq. km)

Legend
● GLACIERS
★ FEATURED GLACIERS BY CONTINENT

WHAT HAVE YOU LEARNED ABOUT GLACIERS?

This map shows the location of glaciers around the world. The largest glaciers by continent also are highlighted. Use this map, and research online to answer these questions.

1. Why does North America have more glaciers than any other part of the world?
2. Which continent has the largest glaciers and why?

EUROPE

ASIA

AFRICA

Siachen Glacier
Continent: Asia
Location: Kashmir
Length: 56 square miles
(144 sq. km)

PACIFIC OCEAN

INDIAN OCEAN

AUSTRALIA

Glaciers of Kilimanjaro
Continent: Africa
Location: Tanzania
Size: 1 square mile
(2.5 sq. km)

SOUTHERN OCEAN

Heard Island Glaciers
Continent: Australia
Location: Australia
Size: 99 square miles
(257 sq. km)

ANTARCTICA

Lambert Glacier
Continent: Antarctica
Size: 15,444 square miles
(40,000 sq. km)

Rocky Road

Most rocks have small cracks. Melted ice from glaciers seeps into the cracks. When the ice freezes again, the rock becomes stuck to the glacier. As the glacier moves, it carries the rock. Glaciers can even pull large boulders out of the ground. When the glacier melts again, the rock is left in a new place. These misplaced rocks are called erratics.

Rocks stuck in glaciers can gouge, or cut, the land with deep grooves as the glacier travels. Gouging changes the landscape.

Sometimes, glaciers gouge valleys near coastlines. Some valley glaciers reach coasts. As the ice melts, the glacier moves back. Sometimes, the glacier leaves behind a fjord. A fjord is a narrow inlet with steep mountains on either side. Glaciers can also gouge the sides of mountains. After many years, the mountaintop can resemble a horn or sharp peak.

As glaciers move, they stretch and twist. Movement causes the ice to crack. The cracks are called crevasses. Crevasses can be more than 100 feet (30 m) deep and more than 60 feet (18 m) wide.

■ As glaciers in Glacier Bay, Alaska, reach the water, chunks of ice up to 200 feet (61 meters) high break off and fall into the water.

Crevasses are the greatest danger to people working on glaciers. Light snow can cover and hide them. People and animals can easily fall into a crevasse. Scientists use crevasses to study Earth. Glacier ice inside crevasses tells scientists what Earth was like hundreds and thousands of years ago.

GLACIER LANDFORMS

Alpine glaciers are found in mountain regions. Continental glaciers cover vast areas of land on the continents. As glaciers move across the land, they create new landforms.

Alpine glaciers erode the land, which creates different landforms. This diagram shows a few of the landforms made by the movement of rock pieces and gravel over the land.

Aretes
Aretes are thin, steep-sided rock ridges that form between two valleys. They form when two glaciers move on either side of a ridge.

Horn
A horn forms when many glaciers erode different sides of a rock. It creates a mountain-like peak.

Medial Moraine
A moraine is a pile of soil and rock. A medial moraine forms when two glaciers join. The soil and rock is left behind in a ridge in the center and on top of the glacier.

Cirque
Cirques are bowl-shaped features that form when a glacier moves back toward a mountain. Snow and ice that form the glacier first build up here.

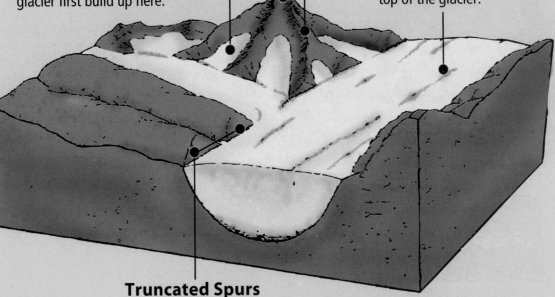

Truncated Spurs
Glaciers tend to follow the flow of a river. When they change course, they can cut off the tops of spurs, truncating, or shortening, them.

In some parts of the world, such as China and South Asia, glaciers provide most of the drinking water. As glaciers retreat, these areas will see a drastic decline in the water available for use by people.

Glacial Deposits and Lakes

Glaciers can carry thousands of small rocks as they travel. On the journey, the rocks break down into smaller pieces. This small, fine-grained material is called rock flour. Rock flour mixes with **sediment** and water. As a glacier melts, it deposits debris called till. A mixture of rock flour, rocks, and other material can be picked up and carried by the glacier. Glacial deposits build up into ridges or piles called moraines.

When glaciers melt, eskers sometimes form. Eskers are former rivers caused by melting water in glaciers that fill with sediment. When the glaciers melt away, large ridges are left behind.

Glaciers can create lakes. Many glacial lakes have formed after glaciers melt into holes in the landscape. The five Great Lakes are former glacial lakes.

One specific type of glacial lake is called a kettle. Kettles form when blocks of ice are buried by glacial debris. The blocks of ice melt very slowly, and a depression, or low area, forms. The depression fills with water, forming a lake. Kettles are usually very small.

■ Glaciers can carry rocks and other materials for hundreds of miles (km). Big Rock, a 16,500-ton (14,969-tonne) boulder in Alberta, Canada, is the largest erratic in the world.

Icebergs

An iceberg is a piece of a glacier that has broken off and floated out to sea. The process of an iceberg breaking off a glacier is called calving. Icebergs can be many miles (km) long. Over time, icebergs melt in warm ocean waters.

Icebergs are dangerous. More than 75 percent of an iceberg is underwater. In 1912, the ship, *Titanic*, struck an iceberg. About 1,513 of the 2,220 passengers on the ship died. Today, coast guards patrol the oceans for icebergs to prevent this from happening again.

The largest icebergs form around Antarctica. The tallest icebergs form in the northern part of the Atlantic Ocean.

What is a Glaciologist?

A glaciologist is someone who studies glaciers. By studying a glacier's growth and shrinkage, a glaciologist learns about Earth's climate.

Lonnie G. Thompson

Lonnie G. Thompson is a glaciologist who works as a professor at The Ohio State University. He is best-known for developing special tools to research the history of ice fields. His studies have helped confirm that global warming is causing glaciers to retreat. Thompson has won many awards, including the National Medal of Science and the Tyler Prize for Environmental Achievement.

Working Conditions
Glaciologists work in freezing conditions. They often sleep in tents in the snow. Sometimes, they work around crevasses.

Tools
Glaciologists use different tools to measure how glaciers change. They take samples of glacial ice called ice cores. Ice cores show the yearly growth of ice layers. Ice cores show when Earth's temperature was warmer or cooler.

Eight Facts About Glaciers

Glaciers cover more than 46,603 square miles (75,000 sq. km) of the United States. Most of these glaciers are located in Alaska.

Only 10 percent of an iceberg can be seen above the water's surface. The remaining 90 percent is below the surface.

There was a secret plan to use icebergs as aircraft carriers during World War II.

Eighty percent of Earth's fresh water is in glaciers.

The core of a glacier remains cold even as the outside heats up.

The remains of woolly mammoths have been found inside glaciers.

Many polar bears live on glaciers. When glaciers melt, it becomes more difficult for polar bears to hunt for food.

Ice crystals found on glaciers can be the size of a baseball.

Glaciers
Brain Teasers

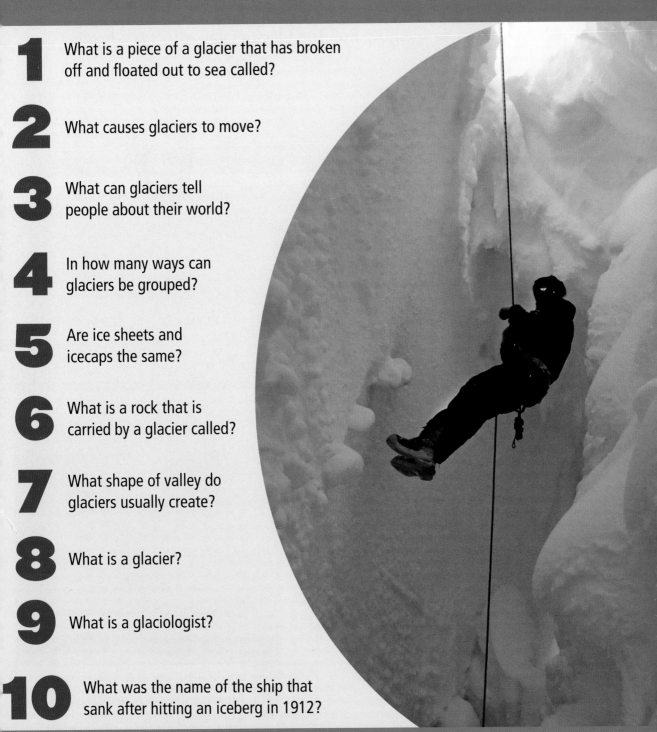

1 What is a piece of a glacier that has broken off and floated out to sea called?

2 What causes glaciers to move?

3 What can glaciers tell people about their world?

4 In how many ways can glaciers be grouped?

5 Are ice sheets and icecaps the same?

6 What is a rock that is carried by a glacier called?

7 What shape of valley do glaciers usually create?

8 What is a glacier?

9 What is a glaciologist?

10 What was the name of the ship that sank after hitting an iceberg in 1912?

ANSWERS: 1. An iceberg **2.** Weight and gravity **3.** Glaciers tell us whether our climate is changing. **4.** Two. Glaciers can be grouped by location and by size. **5.** No. Ice sheets are bigger than icecaps. **6.** An erratic **7.** Glaciers usually gouge U-shaped valleys. **8.** A glacier is a large mass of ice in a very cold region. **9.** Someone who studies ice and snow **10.** *Titanic*

Science in Action

Rising Sea Levels

Try this experiment to see how melting glaciers can affect sea levels.

Tools Needed

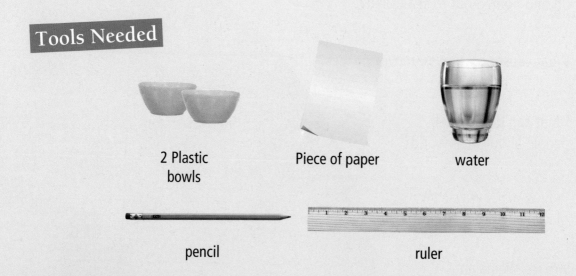

2 Plastic bowls   Piece of paper   water

pencil   ruler

Directions

1 Fill one plastic bowl with water. Place the bowl in the freezer. When the water has completely frozen, pop the ice out of the plastic bowl.

2 Place the frozen block of ice in the second plastic bowl. Slowly add water to the ice until the ice begins to float.

3 With your ruler, measure the level of the water in the bowl. Record your measurement on a piece of paper.

4 Allow the ice to melt completely. Measure the water depth again. Compare your results to the first measurement. Did the "sea" level rise? How do you think melting glaciers can affect the level of water in the oceans?

Words to Know

avalanches: sudden sliding of large masses of snow and rock down a mountain

climates: the usual weather in a region throughout the year

continent: the seven large land masses on Earth; Africa, Antarctica, Asia, Australia, Europe, North America, and South America

erode: remove rock and pieces of soil by natural forces such as water, ice, waves, and wind

evaporates: changes from a liquid or solid to a gas

gravity: the force that pulls objects toward the center of Earth

greenhouse gases: the warming of Earth's surface due to the release of too much carbon dioxide in the air

sediment: very small pieces of rock and dirt deposited by water, wind, or ice

tundra: a flat, treeless region where the ground remains permanently frozen

Index

Log on to www.av2books.com

AV² by Weigl brings you media enhanced books that support active learning. Go to **www.av2books.com**, and enter the special code inside the front cover of this book. You will gain access to enriched and enhanced content that supplements and complements this book. Content includes video, audio, web links, quizzes, a slide show, and activities.

Audio
Listen to sections of the book read aloud.

Video
Watch informative video clips.

Web Link
Find research sites and play interactive games.

Try This!
Complete activities and hands-on experiments.

WHAT'S ONLINE?

Try This! Complete activities and hands-on experiments.	**Web Link** Find research sites and play interactive games.	**Video** Watch informative video clips.	**EXTRA FEATURES**
Pages 6-7 Try this activity about glacier zones	**Pages 10-11** Link to more information about glacier movement	**Pages 4-5** Watch a video about glaciers	**Audio** Hear introductory audio at the top of every page
Pages 10-11 Use this timeline activity to test your knowledge of world events	**Pages 14-15** Find out more about glacier landforms	**Pages 8-9** Check out a video about glacier locations	**Key Words** Study vocabulary, and play a matching word game.
Pages 12-13 See if you can identify glaciers around the world	**Pages 18-19** Learn more about being a glaciologist	**Pages 16-17** View how glaciers shape the land	**Slide Show** View images and captions, and try a writing activity.
Pages 18-19 Write about a day in the life of a glaciologist	**Page 20** Link to facts about glaciers		**AV² Quiz** Take this quiz to test your knowledge
Page 22 Try the activity in the book, then play an interactive game			